LEARN TO DRAW

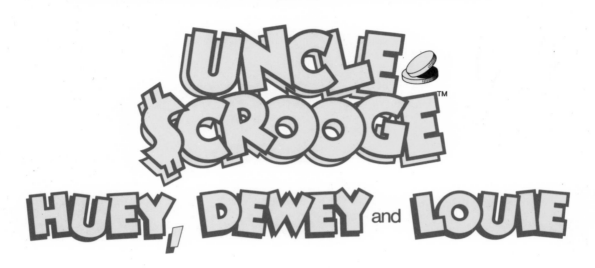

Disney

LEARN TO DRAW

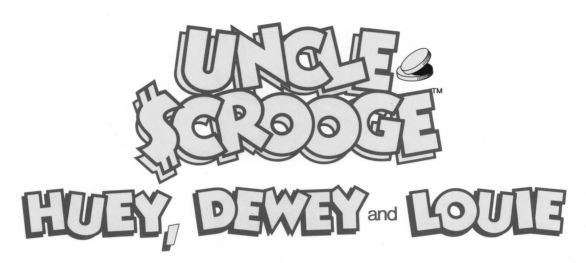

UNCLE $CROOGE
HUEY, DEWEY and LOUIE

Illustrated by
Peter Emslie
Diana Wakeman

Walter Foster

Hi, Gang!

Wouldn't you love to be able to draw Uncle Scrooge and Huey, Dewey, and Louie? It's lots of fun — and easier than you'd believe! First, you'll need some basic art supplies.

OF COURSE, YOU'LL NEED A PENCIL. A NUMBER 2 IS BEST. ALWAYS HAVE A PENCIL SHARPENER ON HAND SO YOU CAN KEEP A SHARP POINT.

YOU'LL NEED PAPER TO DRAW ON — A SKETCH PAD WOULD GIVE YOU A GOOD SUPPLY. AND YOU'LL USE A SOFT ERASER TO REMOVE ANY MISTAKES AND TO CLEAN UP.

UNCA' DONALD

PICK UP A FEW BRUSHES, INCLUDING A LARGE BRUSH TO COLOR IN BROAD AREAS, AND A FINE ONE FOR DETAILS.

YOU'LL USE A BLACK FELT-TIP PEN AS YOU FINISH YOUR PICTURE.

POSTER PAINTS COME IN LOTS OF DIFFERENT COLORS. YOU'LL WANT TO HAVE RED, YELLOW, BLUE, GREEN, ORANGE, PURPLE, BLACK, WHITE, AND BROWN. YOU CAN ADD A FEW MORE IF YOU LIKE — THEY'LL ALL COME IN HANDY.

Getting the Right Shapes

If you can draw these simple shapes, you can draw Uncle Scrooge and Huey, Dewey, and Louie! Practice drawing the lines and shapes, over and over, right on top of each other, until just the right shape appears.

DRAW LINES WITH SMOOTH CURVES AND SHARP CURVES. DRAW LOTS OF CURVES TOGETHER.

LIGHTLY DRAW AROUND AND AROUND UNTIL CIRCLES START TO FORM. DRAW CIRCLES OF DIFFERENT SIZES.

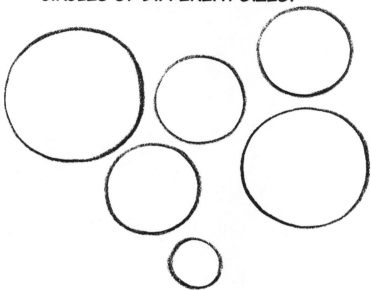

AN OVAL LOOKS LIKE A CIRCLE THAT HAS BEEN STRETCHED OR SQUASHED. DRAW OVALS OF DIFFERENT SHAPES AND SIZES.

DRAW CIRCLES AND CURVED LINES ON TOP OF EACH OTHER. JOIN THEM TO MAKE PEAR SHAPES. DRAW PEAR SHAPES OF DIFFERENT SHAPES AND SIZES.

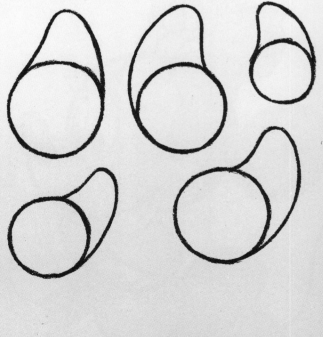

Finishing Off

DEWEY'S USING A NUMBER 2 PENCIL TO SKETCH IN A CIRCLE FOR THE BASIC SHAPE OF SCROOGE'S HEAD. HE'S KEEPING HIS LINES LIGHT AND SMOOTH.

HUEY IS USING AN ERASER TO CAREFULLY REMOVE ANY MISTAKES OR EXTRA LINES, SO THAT THE DRAWING LOOKS NEAT AND CLEAN.

NOW DONALD OUTLINES THE CLEAN PENCIL DRAWING WITH A BLACK FELT-TIP PEN, TAKING TIME TO MAKE SURE HE GETS THOSE LINES JUST RIGHT!

MICKEY IS ADDING THE COLOR WITH HIS BRUSH AND PAINTS, MAKING SURE TO STAY INSIDE THE LINES.

Let's Draw Uncle Scrooge's Head

You can draw Uncle Scrooge's face and head using just a few circles, ovals, and curved lines! The blue lines show each new step of the drawing that you will need to make.

1 START BY DRAWING A CIRCLE FOR UNCLE SCROOGE'S HEAD. ADD A CENTER LINE FROM TOP TO BOTTOM AND CROSS IT WITH ANOTHER LINE ABOUT 1/5 OF THE WAY UP. THESE LINES WILL HELP YOU POSITION THE FEATURES.

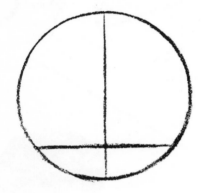

2 DRAW OVALS FOR THE EYES AND PUPILS. THE EYES SHOULD SIT ON THE LINE THAT CROSSES SCROOGE'S HEAD.

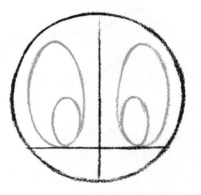

5 USE CURVED LINES TO GIVE THE BILL THICKNESS. TO DRAW SCROOGE'S HAT, START WITH A LARGE CYLINDER SHAPE FITTING OVER HIS HEAD. ADD A SERIES OF CURVES FOR THE BRIM.

6 DRAW THE CURVED HAT BAND, BRIM, AND HIGHLIGHT, AND SHAPE THE SIDEBURNS. DRAW THE TONGUE AND SPECTACLES. ADD TWO SMALL CHEEKS AND TINY SMILE LINES.

Be sure to keep your lines light and smooth. If you make a mistake, use your eraser to remove the unwanted lines.

3 USE CURVED LINES TO MAKE SCROOGE'S UPPER BILL. A SINGLE CURVE CONNECTS THE BOTTOM OF THE EYES. TWO OTHER LINES BEGIN ON THE LOWER SIDES OF THE CIRCLE. THEY CURVE OUT AND BEND IN SHARPLY, JOINING SMOOTHLY IN THE MIDDLE.

4 TO FORM SCROOGE'S LOWER BILL, DRAW A LARGE, BROAD-BASED "V" SHAPE WITH A CURVED, FLATTENED BOTTOM AND TOP IT WITH SHARP CURVES ON BOTH SIDES. ADD MORE CURVES FOR THE BROW RIDGES AND FOR THE BASIC SHAPE OF THE SIDEBURNS.

7 IT'S TIME TO CLEAN UP YOUR DRAWING. CAREFULLY REMOVE ANY UNWANTED LINES WITH YOUR ERASER.

8 OUTLINE YOUR PENCIL DRAWING WITH A BLACK FELT-TIP PEN AND LET THE INK DRY. USE YOUR BRUSH TO PAINT IN THE COLOR — AND YOU'RE DONE!

Let's Draw Huey's Head

You may have noticed that Huey, Dewey, and Louie look quite a bit alike. If you learn to draw one, you can draw them all! Of course you'll want to color them differently as you finish your picture.

1 LIGHTLY DRAW A CIRCLE. THIS IS THE BASIC SHAPE OF HUEY'S HEAD. DRAW A CENTER LINE FROM TOP TO BOTTOM AND CROSS IT WITH ANOTHER LINE ABOUT 1/6 OF THE WAY UP.

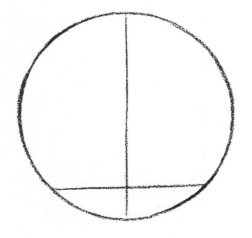

2 DRAW OVALS FOR THE EYES AND PUPILS. BE SURE TO PLACE THE EYES ON THE LINE THAT CROSSES HUEY'S HEAD.

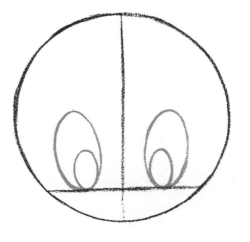

5 USE CURVED LINES TO GIVE THE BILL THICKNESS. USE A SERIES OF CURVES TO FIT A CAP SNUGLY ON HUEY'S HEAD AND TO ADD THE BRIM.

6 DRAW A LINE ON THE HAT TO SEPARATE THE PANELS. ADD THE BUTTON ON TOP. DRAW TINY, CURVED SMILE LINES AT THE CORNERS OF THE MOUTH. ADD SMALL CHEEKS, A "V"-SHAPED TONGUE, AND THREE TUFTS OF HAIR PEEKING OUT FROM BELOW THE CAP'S BRIM.

Remember to draw lightly and smoothly as you follow the steps below. The blue lines show the new steps you will need to draw as we proceed. If you make any mistakes, use your eraser to remove the unwanted lines.

 FOR HUEY'S UPPER BILL, START BY DRAWING A CURVING LINE THAT CROSSES THE CENTER LINE BETWEEN THE EYES. ADD A CURVED LINE AT THE BASE OF THE CIRCLE TO FORM THE UPPER BILL. NOTICE THAT HUEY'S UPPER BILL IS SMALLER THAN SCROOGE'S.

 HUEY'S LOWER BILL IS A BROAD-BASED "V" SHAPE TOPPED ON EACH SIDE BY A SHARP CURVE. THESE CURVES CONNECT TO THE UPPER BILL. ADD CURVED LINES FOR THE BROW RIDGES ABOVE THE EYES.

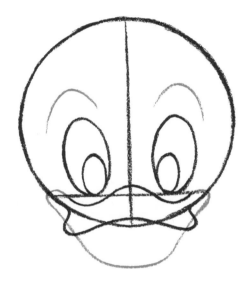

 GENTLY ERASE ANY UNWANTED LINES AND CLEAN UP THE DRAWING.

 USE YOUR BLACK FELT-TIP PEN TO OUTLINE YOUR DRAWING. LET THE INK DRY AND THEN CAREFULLY PAINT IN THE COLOR WITH YOUR BRUSH.

Uncle Scrooge — the 3/4 View

You'll want to be able to draw Uncle Scrooge from a number of angles, not just the front. The vertical center line is now curved in the direction Scrooge is looking, and is pushed over to that side.

1 START WITH A LIGHTLY DRAWN CIRCLE FOR SCROOGE'S HEAD. DRAW THE CURVED CENTER LINE AND ADD A CURVED LINE THAT CROSSES IT ABOUT 1/5 OF THE WAY UP.

2 DRAW OVALS FOR THE EYES ON EITHER SIDE OF THE CENTER LINE. MAKE SURE THAT THE EYES SIT ON THE LINE THAT CROSSES SCROOGE'S HEAD. THE FAR EYE IS SMALLER BECAUSE IT IS PARTLY OUT OF SIGHT AS IT TURNS AWAY FROM US.

5 USE CURVED LINES TO GIVE THICKNESS TO THE BILL. DRAW THE MAIN PART OF SCROOGE'S HAT AS A LARGE CYLINDER SHAPE THAT FITS ON TOP OF HIS HEAD. ADD A SERIES OF CURVES FOR THE BRIM.

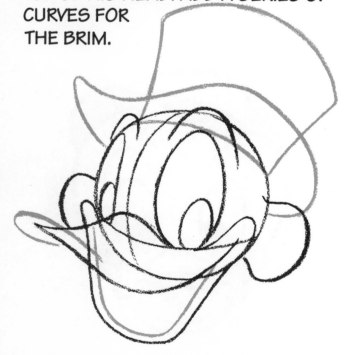

6 DRAW THE CURVED HAT BAND, BRIM, AND HIGHLIGHT. DETAIL THE SIDEBURNS. DRAW THE TONGUE AND OVAL-SHAPED SPECTACLES. ADD THE SMALL CHEEK AND TINY SMILE LINE.

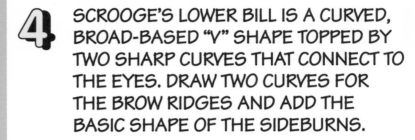

3 USE CURVES TO FORM SCROOGE'S UPPER BILL. ONE CURVE CONNECTS THE BOTTOM OF THE EYES. TWO OTHER CURVED LINES CONNECT IN A POINT OVER TO THE LEFT OF SCROOGE'S HEAD.

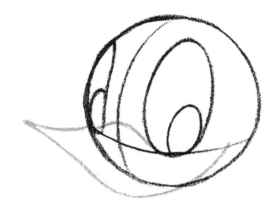

4 SCROOGE'S LOWER BILL IS A CURVED, BROAD-BASED "V" SHAPE TOPPED BY TWO SHARP CURVES THAT CONNECT TO THE EYES. DRAW TWO CURVES FOR THE BROW RIDGES AND ADD THE BASIC SHAPE OF THE SIDEBURNS.

7 USE YOUR ERASER TO CAREFULLY REMOVE THE CONSTRUCTION LINES.

8 OUTLINE YOUR DRAWING WITH YOUR FELT-TIP PEN AND LET THE INK DRY. USE YOUR PAINT AND BRUSHES TO COLOR IN YOUR PICTURE OF SCROOGE.

Dewey —
the 3/4 View

Let's try drawing Dewey turned slightly to the right. You'll see that the center line gets pushed to that side. This will help you to position Dewey's features so that they all point in that direction.

1 DRAW A CIRCLE FOR DEWEY'S HEAD. ADD A CURVED CENTER LINE AND CROSS IT WITH ANOTHER CURVED LINE RUNNING FROM SIDE TO SIDE, ABOUT 1/6 OF THE WAY UP.

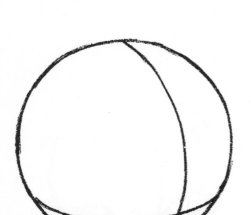

2 USE OVALS TO DRAW THE EYES AND PUPILS ON EITHER SIDE OF THE CENTER LINE. THE EYES SHOULD SIT ON THE LINE THAT CROSSES DEWEY'S HEAD. THE FAR EYE IS SMALLER BECAUSE IT IS FARTHER AWAY FROM US.

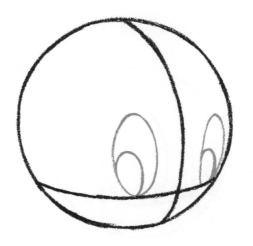

5 USE CURVES TO GIVE THICKNESS TO BOTH THE UPPER AND LOWER BILL. DRAW A SERIES OF CURVED LINES TO FORM DEWEY'S CAP AND BRIM.

6 DRAW A LINE ON THE HAT TO SEPARATE THE PANELS. ADD A BUTTON ON TOP. DRAW A SMILE LINE AT THE CORNER OF HIS MOUTH. ADD A SMALL CHEEK, A "V"-SHAPED TONGUE, AND THREE TUFTS OF HAIR.

 3 DRAW DEWEY'S UPPER BILL USING CURVED LINES. ONE CURVE CROSSES THE CENTER LINE BETWEEN THE EYES. TWO OTHER CURVES CONNECT IN A POINT OVER TO THE RIGHT OF HIS HEAD.

 4 DRAW DEWEY'S LOWER BILL USING A LARGE, BROAD-BASED "V" SHAPE TOPPED ON EACH SIDE BY A SHARP CURVE. THESE CURVES CONNECT WITH THE CURVE OF THE UPPER BILL. ADD THE BROW RIDGES BY DRAWING CURVED LINES ABOVE THE EYES.

 7 USE YOUR ERASER TO GENTLY REMOVE ANY UNWANTED LINES OR STRAY PENCIL MARKS.

 8 OUTLINE YOUR DRAWING WITH A BLACK FELT-TIP PEN, LET THE INK DRY, AND COLOR IN DEWEY!

Uncle Scrooge's Expressions

Uncle Scrooge is a duck with some pretty strong opinions! His eyes, brows, and bill all change shape and position to reflect his different moods.

YOU CAN MAKE A *SLEEPY* UNCLE SCROOGE BY DRAWING EYELIDS THAT SAG HEAVILY OVER HIS PUPILS. DROOPY SIDEBURNS ADD TO THE EFFECT.

UNCLE SCROOGE DOES HAVE A SHORT FUSE! WHEN HE IS *ANGRY*, HIS BROWS ARCH DOWNWARD OVER HIS EYES IN A "V" SHAPE, CREATING A DEEP FURROW IN HIS FOREHEAD.

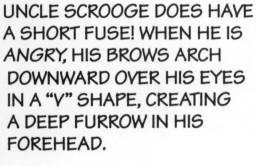

LOUIE'S PUTTING THE FINISHING TOUCHES ON A *SAD* UNCLE SCROOGE. HE'S DRAWN THE BROWS SO THEY ARCH UPWARD, PARTLY AFFECTING THE SHAPE OF THE EYES. HE'S ALSO TURNED SCROOGE'S MOUTH DOWN AT THE CORNERS.

TO DRAW A *SUSPICIOUS* SCROOGE, RAISE ONE EYEBROW AND DIP THE OTHER LOW OVER HIS EYE.

Let's Draw Hands

Louie's showing us the simple steps you'll use to draw Uncle Scrooge's hands. Use the same steps to draw the nephews' hands, but make their fingers and thumbs shorter and stubbier.

1 LIGHTLY DRAW A CIRCLE. ADD A LONG CURVED LINE RUNNING FROM ONE SIDE OF THE CIRCLE TO THE OTHER TO FORM THE BASIC SHAPE OF THE FINGERS. DRAW TWO LINES FOR THE ARM.

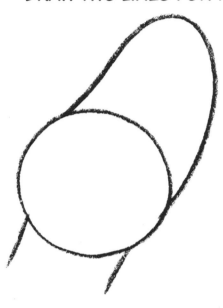

2 USE A CURVING LINE TO ADD THE THUMB TO THE CIRCLE HALFWAY BETWEEN THE WRIST AND THE FINGERS. NOTICE THAT THIS COMPLETES A "MITTEN" SHAPE.

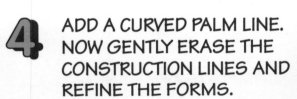

3 SEPARATE THE FINGERS WITH SLIGHTLY CURVING LINES. GIVE THE SHAPE OF THE FINGERS A LITTLE VARIETY TO MAKE THEM LOOK RELAXED AND NATURAL.

4 ADD A CURVED PALM LINE. NOW GENTLY ERASE THE CONSTRUCTION LINES AND REFINE THE FORMS.

Uncle Scrooge Standing

When drawing a full figure, you should begin with the line of action. This is a guideline that will help you to give your character direction and movement.

1

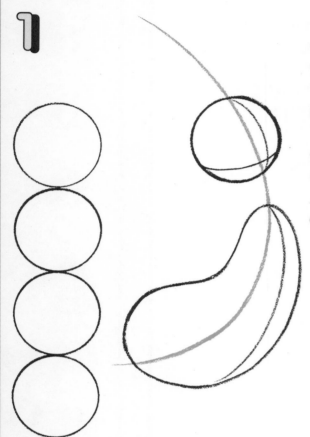

LIGHTLY DRAW THE LINE OF ACTION. DRAW A CIRCLE FOR SCROOGE'S HEAD AND A PEAR SHAPE FOR HIS BODY. NOTICE HOW THE CURVE OF THE PEAR SHAPE FOLLOWS THE LINE OF ACTION. ADD CURVED CENTER LINES.

2

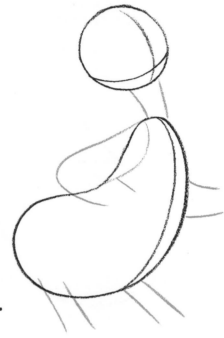

ADD CURVED, TUBE-LIKE SHAPES FOR THE NECK, ARMS, AND LEGS. IN THIS POSE, SCROOGE'S ARMS ARE BENT, FORMING A CREASE ON THE INSIDE OF THE ARM.

5

COMPLETE THE HANDS AS YOU LEARNED BEFORE AND DRAW CREASES WHERE THE TOP OF THE LEG JOINS THE BODY. ADD A CURVED MIDDLE TOE TO EACH FOOT AND GIVE SCROOGE'S TAIL THREE FLUFFY FEATHERS.

6

USING A VARIETY OF CURVED LINES, DRAW THE COAT AND SPATS. YOU'LL NEED A FEW STRAIGHT LINES AND CURVES TO ADD THE CANE THAT FITS SNUGLY IN HIS HAND.

Uncle Scrooge is four heads tall. This means that if you stack four balls the size of Scrooge's head on top of each other, that is how tall he should be.

3

DRAW OVALS FOR THE HANDS AND ROUNDED TRIANGLES FOR THE FEET. FORM THE BEGINNING OF A TAIL WITH TWO SHORT CURVES THAT CONNECT AT A POINT.

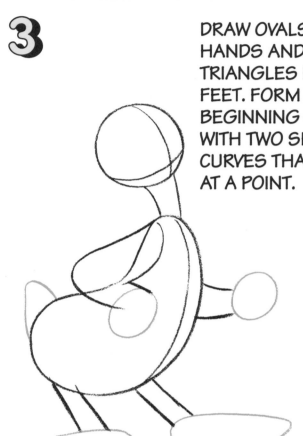

4

USING WHAT YOU'VE ALREADY LEARNED, ADD THE FACIAL FEATURES AND THE HAT.

7

ERASE THE CONSTRUCTION LINES AND CLEAN UP THE DRAWING.

8

OUTLINE YOUR DRAWING WITH YOUR FELT-TIP PEN AND LET THE INK DRY. NOW YOU'RE READY TO COLOR!

Huey Standing

Remember, if you can draw one of the nephews, you can draw them all! Huey is three heads tall. This means that if you stack three balls of equal size on top of each other, that is how tall Huey should be.

1

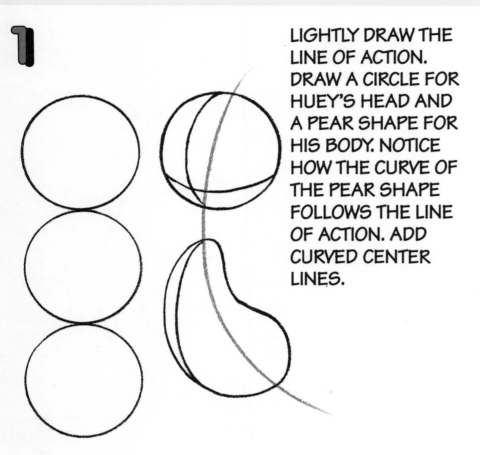

LIGHTLY DRAW THE LINE OF ACTION. DRAW A CIRCLE FOR HUEY'S HEAD AND A PEAR SHAPE FOR HIS BODY. NOTICE HOW THE CURVE OF THE PEAR SHAPE FOLLOWS THE LINE OF ACTION. ADD CURVED CENTER LINES.

2

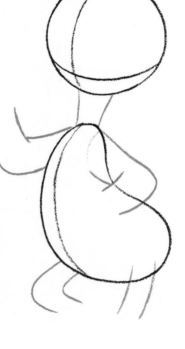

DRAW CURVED, TUBE-LIKE SHAPES FOR HUEY'S NECK, ARMS, AND LEGS. BEND THEM AT THE ELBOWS AND KNEE.

5

COMPLETE THE HANDS AS YOU LEARNED BEFORE AND DRAW CREASES WHERE THE TOP OF THE LEG JOINS THE BODY. ADD A CURVED MIDDLE TOE TO EACH FOOT AND GIVE HUEY'S TAIL THREE FLUFFY FEATHERS.

6

USE CURVED LINES TO DRAW HUEY'S SHIRT. NOTICE HOW THE SLEEVES HANG OFF THE ARMS ON ONE SIDE.

Whatever character you are drawing, if you're showing the full figure, you should always start with the line of action. This is a guideline that will help you to give your character direction and movement.

3 DRAW OVALS FOR THE BASIC SHAPE OF THE HANDS, AND ROUNDED TRIANGLES FOR THE FEET. START THE SHAPE OF THE TAIL WITH TWO SHORT, CONNECTED CURVES.

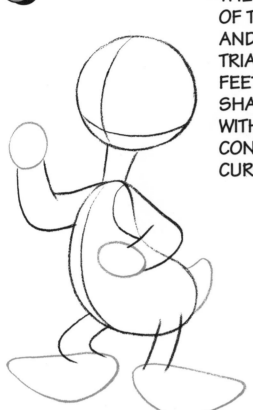

4 ADD THE CAP AND THE FACIAL FEATURES AS YOU LEARNED BEFORE. DRAW LIGHTLY, SO YOU CAN EASILY ERASE MISTAKES AND CONSTRUCTION LINES.

7 CAREFULLY REMOVE THE CONSTRUCTION LINES AND CLEAN UP THE DRAWING WITH YOUR ERASER.

8 USE YOUR FELT-TIP PEN TO OUTLINE YOUR DRAWING OF HUEY. AFTER THE INK DRIES, COLOR HIM IN WITH YOUR BRUSH AND PAINTS.

More Hands

When drawing hands, you may find it useful to use your own hand as a model. But remember to soften the shapes and exaggerate the action in your drawings. Notice how Scrooge's fingers and thumb are longer and less round than Louie's.

The Nephews' Expressions

It's never hard to tell what Huey, Dewey, and Louie are thinking and feeling. Their flexible features stretch and squash to reflect every mood.

WHEN DEWEY'S *CONFUSED*, HE HAS A FURROWED BROW, HIS PUPILS CROSS, AND HIS MOUTH SHUTS TIGHT.

TO DRAW A *BASHFUL* LOUIE, LOWER HIS LIDS SLIGHTLY, MOVE HIS PUPILS TO THE CORNERS OF HIS EYES, AND GIVE HIM A SHEEPISH SMILE.

HUEY LOOKS *STARTLED* WHEN HIS HEAD AND EYES STRETCH UPWARD, HIS MOUTH DROPS OPEN, AND HIS HAT GOES FLYING OFF HIS HEAD!

IT LOOKS AS IF HUEY WANTS TO TAKE A TURN MAKING UP SOME NEW EXPRESSIONS. HOW ABOUT YOU?

Scrooge Walking
Dewey Running

To make your characters come alive you'll have to make them move! The line of action is particularly important in giving a moving figure the direction and motion he needs.

1

LIGHTLY DRAW THE LINE OF ACTION. ADD A CIRCLE FOR SCROOGE'S HEAD AND A PEAR SHAPE FOR HIS BODY. DRAW IN THE CURVED CENTER LINES. ADD SCROOGE'S TUBE-LIKE NECK, ARMS, AND LEGS. ADD OVALS FOR THE HANDS, AND ROUNDED TRIANGLES FOR THE FEET. ADD THE BASIC TAIL SHAPE.

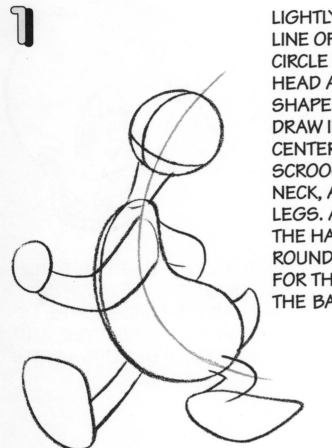

2

DRAW IN THE DETAILS FOR THE FACE, HAND, FEET, AND TAIL AS YOU LEARNED TO DO EARLIER.

1

DRAW THE LINE OF ACTION AND BASIC CONSTRUCTION, USING CURVED LINES, OVALS, AND ROUNDED TRIANGLES, AS YOU'VE DONE BEFORE.

2

DRAW IN THE DETAILS FOR THE FACE, HANDS, BODY, FEET, AND TAIL.

Notice how arms and legs become more extended when you draw Dewey running than when you show Scrooge out for a stroll.

3 ADD IN UNCLE SCROOGE'S JACKET, SPATS, HAT, AND CANE.

4 REMOVE THE CONSTRUCTION LINES AND CLEAN UP THE DRAWING WITH YOUR ERASER. OUTLINE UNCLE SCROOGE WITH A BLACK FELT-TIP PEN AND LET THE INK DRY. NOW COLOR HIM IN!

 ADD DEWEY'S SHIRT AND CAP, USING CURVED LINES.

 ERASE THE CONSTRUCTION LINES. USE YOUR FELT-TIP PEN TO OUTLINE THE DRAWING. WHEN THE INK IS DRY, COLOR IN DEWEY!

More Action Poses

NOTICE THE EXAGGERATION IN THIS POSE AS SCROOGE'S HEAD TILTS BACK TO ADMIRE THE VERY FIRST PENNY HE EVER EARNED!

SCROOGE IS HEADED OFF TO THE BANK AGAIN! THE MOVEMENT IN THIS POSE IS HEIGHTENED BY THE WAY HE PUSHES OFF WITH ONE FOOT AND POINTS HIS CANE.

NOTICE HOW THE LINE OF ACTION BECOMES HORIZONTAL WHEN A CHARACTER IS SWIMMING, SKYDIVING, OR JUST LYING DOWN.

Try drawing Uncle Scrooge and the nephews in the activities below. Then make up some yourself.

LOUIE'S BODY LEANS FORWARD, BUT HIS HEAD TILTS BACK. THIS CAN BE SEEN IN THE LINE OF ACTION. THE LITTLE MOTION LINES AROUND THE BASKETBALL ADD AN ANIMATED EFFECT.

LAUGHTER IS CONVEYED NOT ONLY BY THE FACE, BUT ALSO BY THE BODY. HUEY LEANS FORWARD, WITH ONE HAND POINTING AND THE OTHER ON HIS KNEE.

POW! DEWEY'S PUT SO MUCH ENERGY INTO HIS KICK THAT HIS WHOLE BODY IS THROWN BACKWARD.

Coloring Tips

HUEY AND DEWEY ARE TAKING
A DIFFERENT APPROACH BY ADDING
THE COLOR TO THEIR PICTURE
OF UNCLE SCROOGE FIRST,
AND THEN DRAWING THE OUTLINE
WITH THEIR FELT-TIP MARKER.
WHY DON'T YOU GIVE THIS TECHNIQUE
A TRY?

YOU CAN CREATE JUST ABOUT ANY COLOR IN THE WORLD IF YOU MIX YOUR PAINTS ON A PALETTE (OR A WASHABLE PLATE), AS LOUIE IS DOING HERE.

IT LOOKS AS IF DONALD DIDN'T WASH OUT HIS BRUSH BEFORE THE PAINT DRIED AND RUINED THE BRISTLES. BE SURE *YOU* TAKE *GOOD* CARE OF YOUR BRUSHES. IF YOU DO, THEY'LL LAST A LONG TIME.

Other Ways To Color

It's fun to try other materials and techniques to finish your pictures.

MICKEY IS USING A SET OF COLORED PENCILS TO COLOR IN HIS PORTRAIT OF HUEY.

MARKERS WILL MAKE A BRIGHT AND COLORFUL PICTURE, TOO.

PLUTO IS ADDING COLOR TO A DRAWING OF DEWEY WITH A BRUSH AND A TRAY OF WATERCOLORS.